MORE TIME MORE FUNDS

100 Methods to increase your time and your income

ISBN: 9798847339520

Disclaimer

For the purpose of educating readers about Internet marketing, this e-book was prepared. This e-book has been meticulously edited and proofread to ensure its accuracy and completeness. On the other hand, there can be grammatical or substance errors. Also, the material in this e-book is only current as of the time of publication. As a result, this e-book should only be used as a guide and not as the sole source of information.

This e-book's main objective is to impart knowledge. The content in this e-book is not guaranteed to be accurate and up-to-date by the author or the publisher, who also disclaim any liability for any typographical or other errors. In regards to any loss or damage caused or alleged to have been caused directly or indirectly by this e-book, the author and publisher shall have no liability for such damages and shall not be held responsible to any person or entity.

The book More Time, More Funds: 100 Ways to Get More Time & Earn More Funds

Have you gotten weary and fed up with working ten to twelve hours a day and making hardly more than the minimum wage?
If you're like many people, you can feel as though your workstation has taken on the characteristics of a prison cell that has kept you all sequestered from the rest of society. And yet, you continue to find yourself surviving paycheck to paycheck. Time, they claim that it is money.
If that's the case, it emphasizes the fact that other people are undoubtedly generating a whole lot more money in the same amount of time you are ready to put in, or perhaps at a very far lesser time.

You've probably already come to the conclusion that there must be a more effective technique to engage in the game of earning money.
Yes. In actuality, there are a hundred various ways that the game can be played that are better.

It's feasible to work less hours and still make more money. You've observed other folks doing it. Now is the moment to write your own success story and make it come true in your life.

Finding a significantly better approach to play the game could potentially get you twenty times or more return, but boosting production will only increase your return by a factor of two.
Success, according to Robert Collier, "is the total of tiny efforts, repeated day in and day out,"
Whenever you discover a more effective method of carrying out a task, whether it be a quicker approach to obtain a pay increase or a more time-saving method, it is a great accomplishment.

Precisely because your time has increased in value and is now worth more money, you are able to earn more by taking a powerful method to sifting through your daily emails.
However, the real issue is how exactly do you go about doing that. How can you get to the point where you work less yet make more money?
The "secrets" to increasing your income are actually everywhere around you. There's a good chance that your neighbors down the street are making a fortune doing stuff you'd never even consider.
Time is money, they say.
It's time you learned how successful individuals spend their important time.

1. Discover the affiliate programs' possibilities for financial gain.
Setting up a website that pre-sells company products is one common and very efficient technique to

generate passive income. In this arrangement, the business provides the goods along with the computer code that keeps track of sales, and you are paid a commission for each one that is successful. Find businesses that are recognized to offer larger commissions and look for customers who are very likely to make numerous purchases over a lengthy period of time, which will result in recurring commissions.

2. Publish informational products, such as eBooks. An eBook that offers "How To" information, such as How to Start Your Online Business, or any other topic intended to provide information on how to make people's lives easier, is a valuable resource available on the web and may be easily created and sold there. Information is in extremely high demand, which is something you can take advantage of. The amazing thing about eBooks is that they're simpler to make and take less time to finish. Once that is done, all you need to do is create a website, get web hosting, and set up your own internet marketing. This will enable your eBooks to be bought whenever you want, day or night, for numerous years.

3. Generate passive residual money by paying advertising commissions.
If you have or plan to have a website, work on attracting visitors or creating web traffic by offering pertinent, unique, and up-to-date information to

entice people to visit your sites. You can expect to receive recurring passive revenue each month by allowing advertisers to display banners or links on your website in exchange for a charge.

4. Establish yourself as a provider of domain registration or web hosting services.
Offer a monthly subscription-based web hosting solution that you can then resell to consumers for a set subscription fee. To ensure that your customers receive timely and dependable support, it is crucial that you are completely aware with and informed about the web hosting service if you intend to offer this kind of service.

5. Understand the fine art of compensation negotiating.
Instead of waiting for the money topic to come up during a job interview, you can bring it up yourself and ask the interviewer/recruiter what the anticipated salary range is for the position you are applying for. Since you already know the numbers and can decide in advance if it's something viable enough for you to pursue your application, you won't have to waste time going back and forth during discussions.

6. Make sure your emails are succinct and to the point.

Keep everything brief and to the point rather than wasting time on lengthy emails. To begin with, your subject line ought to be enlightening so that your audience can decide whether it is something they should prioritize. Avoid using the passive voice while expressing your ideas clearly.

7. By simply asking people if they have a problem you can help resolve, you can effectively generate business and sales leads.
For instance, if you are providing web design services, ask straight questions instead of gauging interest in a new website, like "Who among you isn't content with their present website?" This significantly shortens the response-seeking process and allows you to save time.

8. 80% accuracy is usually sufficient when working as a team.
You probably already know that time is money, and large projects typically have time limits. 80% accuracy is usually always sufficient when working in a team. You can save the remaining 20% for the practice or testing stage, where you can iron out the finer points. It's important to remember that finishing the job quickly and well is more crucial than paying attention to every last detail.

9. Speak with an actual member of customer service staff.
When contacting customer care, speaking with a live person on the other end of the phone instead of an automated system will result in a quicker and more effective resolution. Try checking contacthelp.com or gethuman.com to see if there is a code for the particular company you need to call in order to avoid the automated systems if you have an urgent or significant issue.

10. The ability to say "no" is a skill that you should master.
Consider your workload at the moment and be mindful of your limits before making any commitments. Not only will developing the ability to say no free up your time, but it will also relieve a lot of tension from your life. People that are successful have no issue making decisions, putting their foot down on something, and saying no because they know what they want.

11. Master the skill of delegation.
Keep in mind that you do not have enough time in the day to do and attend to everything if you are the type of person who is used to doing everything on your own or you find it difficult to let go. Every manager and leader should understand and embrace this crucial value. By learning to delegate responsibilities, you may lessen your workload and increase efficiency.

12. Conduct research to get training in a specialized field.
These days, having a highly sought-after and specialized skill set might make you more valuable as an employee than just an average one. Examine the most valuable and in-demand talents in your sector to see if you can learn to gain them in your leisure time.

13. Achieve a higher education credential or degree.
For you to be eligible for a higher pay scale in some employment areas, you may need to possess a specific degree, certificate, or other form of specialized training. While taking this path could be expensive and time-consuming, it can improve your qualifications and make you eligible for promotions or higher designations, which can turn out to be a worthwhile and profitable investment in the long run. Examine whether investing in night classes and seminars can prove to be a financially sound investment, regardless of whether you're pursuing an MBA or a Six Sigma Black Belt. Take the time to talk about this with the human resources department at your employer because some businesses will pay for suitable employees to continue their education.

14. You might think about modifying your work schedule or working remotely.
Try to negotiate altering your work hours or bring up telecommuting opportunities with your employer if they are unable or unwilling to pay you more for the work you do. It might not be feasible for some businesses, but if you can work primarily from home, it's worth requesting. You can also assess your working hours to see if taking on an additional shift might increase productivity or give you more time to pursue additional income--generating endeavors.

15. Consider working as an independent consultant rather than a full-time employee.
If you frequently work more than the required 40 hours per week, you might want to consider becoming an hourly consultant if it makes more financial sense. Even though you might not work any less, you will have more flexibility with your work schedule, allowing you to take on more customers and make more money rather than working full--time without receiving overtime compensation.

16. If your work is getting better or you are making a bigger contribution, ask for a pay increase.
Ask for a raise based on your performance if you believe you deserve it given the amount of profit you are generating for your firm or the fact that you are working beyond your original job description.

You can time your request for a raise to come right after a performance evaluation. The management won't mind paying you more if you turn out to be a fantastic asset to the business.

17. Find a method that works well for performing repetitive chores.
Try to determine how you can automate or streamline the entire process if your job or daily activities demand you to perform repeated actions on a regular basis. There are numerous software programs and web tools available that are made to eliminate the minute details. Take use of the free apps available to you because they can drastically reduce the time it takes to finish a given task. If you decide it's time to invest in paid software, talk to the management about it and be prepared to provide justifications for the cost. The productivity, accuracy, and efficiency that can be considerably increased by using this program

18. Take into account switching jobs or undertaking a risky career move.
Consider looking for better alternatives if you believe your career is at a standstill and there is no way to leave your current position and shift to one that is more gratifying and promotes a healthier work-life balance. Identify a new workplace where your qualifications and experience are highly regarded. The final line is that you should take action if you are overworked and underpaid.

19. You might think about working as a freelance writer.
You could wish to look for options for freelance writing jobs if you have a knack for writing or a strong command of proper grammar, communication, and spelling. In order to supplement your income, you might submit articles to local periodicals including newspapers, magazines, and blogs. As you go toward creating credibility, gradually expand your portfolio.

20. Teach someone a language.
Do you possess the ability to speak another language? Or perhaps you possess a solid grasp of the English language that would make you a qualified English teacher? This is a highly sought-after expertise that offers excellent prospects for earning money.

21. Carry out online research projects.
You might offer your services as an online researcher to nearby companies if you are certain that you are familiar with the internet.

22. Start working as a "green" consultant.
People are eager to adjust their lifestyles in a way that will result in their using less energy in their homes. By assessing homes and offering advice on how to go "green," you may make a sizable profit in

this enormous sector. Additionally, you can eventually market your services to businesses.

23. Offer organic food for sale.
Consider selling organic produce if you enjoy gardening and are knowledgeable about organic practices. You can provide "in season" organic veggies and fresh herbs to restaurants, depending on the size of your harvest. The tastiest and freshest ingredients are always sought after by chefs, so they constantly monitor their sources.

24. Offer vintage and antique items for sale on eBay.
If you are knowledgeable about antiques, spend your weekends looking through thrift shops, garage sales, and flea markets where you could find precious antiquities for cheap. Get some information by doing some research, then auction it off on eBay.

25. Earn money while you shop.
Many businesses really employ individuals to engage in "mystery shopping" and relay their findings to other businesses.
You must be fair and have a solid grasp of the industry when working in this line of work.

26. Dress up the cakes.
If you enjoy baking, you may make a little extra cash by making and decorating cakes. Show off your baking skills by offering to create pastries and

other treats for area coffee shops, delis, and workplace break rooms.

27. Jams and jellies should be made and sold.
If you know how to make jams and jellies the old-fashioned manner, you may can and preserve them, making it possible to manufacture a significant quantity of jams and jellies that you can sell when they are in season. You have the option of selling it to your friends and coworkers, a nearby market, or even online.

28. Sell your images to earn money.
Offer your services to special occasions like weddings, parties, and business gatherings if you have a fancy camera and a knack for shooting beautiful pictures. Additionally, you can publish them on websites online and earn money each time a user chooses to download and use them.
29. Give yourself some time to organize your savings.
You must ensure that all of your savings are actively working to generate income if you want to gain additional money. Get a fixed-rate account if you have a lump sum of money that you are willing to save for at least a year.

30. Invite a lodger over.
How about making your house work for you and generate its own income instead of spending a fortune to buy a house like most people do? If you have a spare room, you might want to think about renting it out to supplement your income.

31. A parking place can be rented out.
It's a proverbial goldmine right under your nose if you live close to the city center, or near a football stadium or railway station, and you have a garage or parking space that you don't precisely utilize. Earn some additional cash on the side by renting out your parking space to concert or sporting event attendees or commuters.

32. Sell things on eBay.
You're familiar with the adage that anything that one person may consider trash may become treasure to another. Consider selling some of your excess, unneeded items on eBay to raise some cash if they are taking up permanent residence in your basement and taking up too much space in your house.

33. Respond to paid surveys. You can participate in a variety of online surveys where you can earn cash or gift cards in exchange for sharing your ideas.

34. Provide online assistance services.
Today, there are an increasing number of web-based enterprises, and as a result, there is a huge demand for virtual assistance services. Many businesses and individuals employ a virtual assistant's services to carry out research, do time-consuming tasks, find items, make calls, etc.

35. Become financially successful by running an internet forum.
Software like SebFlipper has the capacity to host multiple distinct forums on a single server. By charging forum owners or administrators for your hosting services, you can earn money. Additionally, you can provide this service without charge and advertise your products and services on their message boards to make money.

36. Create podcasts.
Similar to voice or video blogging, where you can talk about certain intriguing subjects and earn money from the commercials shown, this allows you to talk about the things you find interesting. Through this platform, you can connect with hundreds of subscribers if you have a gift for communication and believe you can offer insightful information or captivating opinions.

37. Make an advance plan for the day, then follow it.
You will discover that you are better equipped to face problems and deflect concerns with greater ease if you try planning out your day and anticipating the potential roadblocks. By doing this, you can be sure that your day will be more productive.

38. Divide your ambitious goals into smaller, more doable benchmarks.
Make an effort to accomplish something valuable each day. Your incentive to stay on task and avoid procrastination will increase if you write down your goals, set deadlines, and create calendars.

39. Starting your day by completing the more challenging and time-consuming duties comes highly recommended.
Before progressively moving on to simpler tasks, take advantage of the moment while you still have all of your energy to complete everything.

40. Acquire the skills necessary to respond to disruptions in a decisive and aggressive way. Do not let other people's unimportant worries divert your attention from your goals. This does not necessary imply that you should act in a harsh and disrespectful manner. Instead of continually having to take into account the worries of other people, learn to remain firm and prioritize the crucial things.

41. Quit putting off important tasks.
You should practice not wasting time fretting or procrastinating because doing so just makes you less productive. Keep in mind that time is money. Schedule your "worry time" at the end of each day if you are prone to being paralyzed by worry. This will help you maintain your attention while addressing unfinished business and more pressing issues.

42. Organize your clutter.
Organize your workspace to ensure that everything is where it belongs. This will prevent you from having to spend time looking for lost objects. Productivity can be considerably increased by keeping a clean workstation.

43. Keep your priorities in mind.
Do not develop the habit of postponing or canceling tasks that you can complete right now. While it's possible to claim, "You still have time tomorrow," it just means that there will be a whole new set of difficulties to overcome.

44. Become proficient at batch processing.
All the unimportant, minor, and clerical jobs should be grouped together. Bundle or batch them together and complete them one set at a time rather than running back and forth throughout the day taking care of little things that just serve to disrupt and divert you from more essential duties. With only a

few hours left in your workday, you can make a list of all the tiny activities you need to complete and then start working through them as rapidly as you can. Then, you can cross each job off your list.

45. Brown bagging it

Making and bringing your own lunch to work won't exactly change your life, but it will save you money you wouldn't otherwise have to spend, allow you to work through lunch to gain more time, and offer you more control over what you eat.

46. Take on jobs with a lot of visibility.

Your achievements won't make you a star or get you very far if you are continuously laboring on the sidelines, doing less essential tasks.

Instead, make an effort to volunteer for bigger initiatives because those are the ones that will help you make a name for yourself and promote the business. Consider creating your own project if there aren't any great ones available but you have the knowledge and confidence to complete them. If you succeed, these significant and high-profile projects could have a profound effect on both your profession and your personal life. These are the achievements that can help you build a stronger portfolio.

47. Invest the increase in your pay.
Don't immediately start planning how you'll spend your newfound income if you finally received a raise. Refrain from expanding your spending. As an alternative, think about depositing the entire sum in the bank.

48. Files and workstation should be organized with care.
Even while it is said that creative people can order their own chaos, it can nonetheless cause stress and reduce productivity. Papers and documents that can be discarded should be discarded, and folders should be appropriately labeled.

49 Organize your to-do list.
Examine each item on your to-do list, if it is more than a mile long, and decide which are not necessary. Create the habit of getting rid of things that aren't necessary and start to simplify your life.

50. Eliminate any distractions.
Remove all of the unneeded interruptions, including Twitter and other social networking sites, email and instant messaging alerts, and these. In fact, you might want to think about turning off the Internet if at all possible. You can also wear headphones to block out background workplace noise.

51. Meetings should go no longer than 30 minutes. Meetings that might be completed with a phone call or email are among the most frequent and significant time wasters. When it's possible, ask to be excused from meetings, or if you have the last say, cut them short if they aren't really necessary.

52. Try not to check your email more often than once or twice a day.
You should refrain from continuously checking your email during the day. Schedule a time to go through your mail each day at the beginning of the day, then check again an hour before you leave. Sending pointless emails again and over again can cause recipients to get seriously distracted and will have an impact on everyone's productivity, including your own.

53. Whenever you are at home, turn off the television.
Reducing your television viewing is one of the best methods to save time and money. As a result, you will have more time on your hands to take care of more crucial matters or pursue a more fulfilling activity in place of all those guilt-inducing advertisements.

54. Examine your personal collection to see which items you may part with and sell.
Analyze everything with a critical eye to see if there are any duplicates or anything you're ready to part with. While you're at it, how about thinking about reducing the amount of time you spend on your passion and searching for more lucrative endeavors? It would be wonderful if you had a lucrative pastime or could make money doing what you love. Who knows, this might provide you access to a ton of fantastic chances.

55. When thinking about buying something, always remember the 30-day rule.
If you are tempted to treat yourself to the newest gadget or indulge in a splurge, wait 30 days before asking yourself if you actually need the item. When you wait and resist the need to act immediately, the urge frequently disappears and you wind up saving yourself a considerable sum of money. It's crucial to instill in oneself the habit of forgoing pointless purchases in order to put your money toward financially smart ventures instead.

56. Spending too much money on your kids' entertainment should be avoided.
Focus on developing your child's inventiveness and teaching him to appreciate straightforward and exciting games rather than giving in to the desire to buy him the newest video game or the coolest device on the market. It's crucial for parents to

understand that kids don't need expensive toys to be content; instead, spend more time with them creating things and learning new things to create wonderful memories. You will undoubtedly discover that these options are more beneficial and affordable.

57. Make contact with your credit card company and then request a rate decrease.
Call the company number on the back of any of your cards that have a balance. You should bargain for a lower interest rate if you don't want to consider moving your business elsewhere. Ask for the supervisor if the individual you are speaking to is unable to fulfill your request. If your amount is $5,000 and your interest rate is 3%, you might theoretically save $150 a year.

59. Decide on term life insurance.
Many individuals think that buying insurance is like making an investment. No, it is not. Change to term insurance and utilize the difference in cost to pay off some bills or begin saving. Policies that cover the entire world are substantially more expensive. Instead of spending more money on inferior investments, it is unquestionably preferable to get yourself out of debt.

60. Focus on a car's dependability and fuel efficiency while purchasing one.
Choosing a more fuel-efficient and dependable car will save you thousands of dollars in the long run instead of opting for what's more fashionable or flashier. For instance, buying a car with a 25-mile per gallon fuel economy over one with a 15-mile per gallon fuel economy will save 2, 133 gallons of gasoline over the course of 80, 000 miles of driving. Therefore, if a gallon costs $3, it represents an incredible $ 6, 400 in savings. Do your study and keep in mind that dependability can also yield tremendous rewards. You will receive a significant reward for your efforts.

61. Try to avoid visiting businesses and shopping malls for leisure purposes.
Allowing yourself to indulge in the need to window shop will simply push you to spend more money on items that you don't actually need. Instead, look for other venues to pass the time, such a museum, a park, or a friend's house. You will be better off if you avoid using retail therapy as a substitute for enjoyment.

62. Consider making a little company investment and using a business strategy that has a great chance of making you wealthy.
If you haven't guessed it, entrepreneurs start their own businesses because they long ago came to the realization that a 9 to 5 job would not make them

wealthy. However, starting a business involves meticulous planning, so be sure to think about everything. Establish a strong business concept first. If you don't envision yourself making thousands or millions of dollars from your business idea, you might want to look into other options.

63. Consider carefully identifying and isolating your primary strengths before deciding to build on them. Find a hobby or activity that you actually enjoy; this is a strength you might be able to develop and invest in. It is best to start a business in an area where you can express your abilities so that you can further develop them via practice. This approach has been successfully used by numerous people to reap significant financial rewards. See if you qualify to receive compensation for yours.

64. Decide to work in a field where there is a lot of demand and a healthy profit margin.
After deducting the cost of providing the commodity or service, the difference between the quantities of sales you generate and the money you keep from each sale is how much profit you make. A smaller number of sales will be required to reach the million dollar mark if your margin is higher. Be sure to first determine the potential profit margin of the goods or services you intend to sell before starting any business.

65. Decide to pay with cash.
Paying cash for any non-bill expenses like gas, dining out, and groceries is preferable to routinely charging your purchases to your credit or debit cards. Why? Cash transactions enhance the reality of the purchasing process. Additionally, by choosing to spend cash, you may better regulate your expenditures and avoid going overboard.

66. Make a few little weekly deposits to your savings.
Make an effort to take a few dollars each week out of your available funds. You can start by adding $20 or $40 every week to your savings. Although it's only a small amount, you might maybe not even notice it and still wind up saving a lot of money.

67. Decide against leaving the house and staying there.
You will be tempted to eat at restaurants, fill up at the gas station, visit the mall, and other temptations if you go out, which will urge you to spend money that you don't need to. When you are traveling, it is difficult, if not nearly impossible, to avoid spending, so remain home and look for alternative forms of free amusement. Additionally, you can use this free time to catch up with your loved ones.

68. Steer clear of receiving catalogs or any other email announcements.
These companies created all of these emails and newsletters with the intention of selling you products. It might be incredibly tempting to buy upscale goods or services when you constantly receive notifications of intriguing new releases or impending deals. In order to avoid having to cope with trying to resist temptation, decide to terminate all of your catalog and newsletter subscriptions.

69. Decide to prepare meals at home rather than going out to dine.
It could be challenging to accomplish this, especially if you are too exhausted to prepare food after a long day at work. Throw in a quick stir fry with fresh or frozen vegetables instead of spending money on elaborate dinners, ordering deliveries, or ordering unhealthy takeout or fast food. Cooking homemade and healthier meals doesn't have to be a huge hassle because you can do some advance study on some simple, 10-minute recipes.

70. When separating your money, using the envelope approach.
The same principle of paying with cash is being used here. Divide your available funds into the various categories using envelopes. When you have used up all of your allotment in one envelope, you have completed the task.

71. Discover the spreadsheet tracker trick.
You can manage your funds more effectively by using one of the many pricey programs like Quicken, MS Money, etc. Even if you don't really need all the bells and whistles that merely add to the cost, you don't really need to invest in any of that sophisticated software. Instead, you may monitor your bank account using Google Docs and Spreadsheets. Each transaction has a date field where you may enter the date, along with the transaction's title, amount, and a small field for any notes or memoranda. You can also enter the running balance in this field.

72. Make the decision to pay off debt and savings first.
Every time you get down to pay your bills, either to put money toward savings first or to assign that money to savings first, then pay off your debt. You will commonly choose to underspend it if you consistently decide to save money from what is left over. Decide to spend your savings before anything else. This will enable you to reduce your spending in an efficient manner.

73. Do away with cable television.
Many individuals watch too much television, which is an unproductive hobby. Instead of paying money on a cable subscription, you can choose to download or rent DVDs online, which will allow you to focus on watching the movies that are actually worth

watching rather than wasting time watching the majority of the time-wasting TV programming.

74. Make the decision to use internet savings instead of conventional bank savings accounts.
There are several online banks that provide interest rates that are two times higher than those of traditional banks. However, you won't be given an ATM account or a handy means to withdraw money. Of course, this could be advantageous for you since you could successfully reduce your propensity to make impulsive purchases.

75. Decide to pursue happiness in life rather than through consumption.
Many people make the decision to purchase items because they erroneously believe that doing so will enable them to experience enduring enjoyment. These are the buyers who are constantly driven by a desire to own the newest technology, the most expensive vehicle, or the most fashionable pair of shoes. In actuality, you will only be content with your purchase for one or two days at most when you make a purchase. After that, you'll feel the urge to purchase more, and the vicious cycle will continue indefinitely. Instead, make the decision to cherish and appreciate life. You can decide to find joy in the world around you and in the people you interact with, or perhaps in engaging in activities you truly enjoy. There are a lot of things in life that you can

do to increase your pleasure without having to spend any money.

76. Transform your pastime into a successful business.
It would be foolish to turn off the opportunity to pursue a passion project that will bring in money. If you enjoy experimenting with web design, polish your skills and think about making money from your creativity by taking on logo and web design tasks on the side. If you enjoy riding, you can supplement your income by repairing and maintaining bicycles. People who enjoy baking might make a modest fortune by selling their goods or expensive cookware sets.

77. Use credit cards wisely by developing strategic usage.
To get the most out of utilizing credit cards, pick the card that best suits your spending style. Select credit cards that offer reward points for spending money on items that you typically do. Consequently, make an effort to research which card is best to use for each purchase rather than just using one because it is accessible.

78. Take into account paying for testing.
Become a compensated tester. Many medical and cosmetic corporations pay testers to use their treatments and products firsthand. You will be

required to fulfill a specific set of conditions in order to be eligible.

79. Donate plasma by blood donation.
Unbeknownst to many, blood plasma has a comparatively high level of demand as a commodity. It's excellent that you can donate blood plasma twice in a week as long as there are at least two days between each donation. For each pint, you can often expect to receive between $20 and $35.

80. Understand how to get money by recycling.
To see whether there are any recycling facilities in your area, try looking them up. There are numerous communities with scrap metal recycling facilities, and you can get paid for each pound of metal you bring in. Additionally, rather than discarding glass bottles if you live in a place where you must pay a deposit for each one, decide to return them to receive the deposit. Remember though that doing this beyond state boundaries is prohibited.

81. Try your hand at some unusual jobs.
If you have the skills and experience necessary to complete repairs, clean-ups, or yard work, you may guarantee quick money by selling your services for such tasks. In reality, if you have a truck, you may

offer your services to remove debris and, if done frequently, earn a sizable sum of money.

82. Receive a promotion.
The next best thing you can do is earn that raise by gaining a work promotion if you are not at all comfortable with the thought of asking for a salary increase. It is a universally acknowledged truth that you should expect to be paid more if you work harder. So how about putting in some effort to advance your job and obtain that promotion? Of course, doing well would entail taking thc required actions to subtly emphasize your accomplishments. Nevertheless, you should determine whether there is indeed room for expansion within your organization. You might want to consider setting your sights on something else if a promotion and a pay increase appear out of your reach.

83. On Etsy. Market your handmade goods.
If you are creative, you can open an online business on Etsy and sell your goods there. Many consumers today prefer customized and distinctive products, from handmade wedding invitations to decorative items. Check out many creative DIY ideas you may use at Pinterest.com.

84. You should alter the way you think about and feel about money.
As an employer, you receive payment in exchange for the services you provide. When you are an

entrepreneur, you make money by marketing and providing certain goods and services. Contrary to popular belief, money is not the cause of all evils. It is not, however, a cure-all for all of your woes as well as the ills and issues that plague the entire planet. Money is merely an instrument—a tool that enables you to follow the lifestyle you like while also allowing you to achieve a particular quality of living.

85. The way you think about yourself needs to change.
Running balance or monthly income cannot be used to judge a person's character. You must, however, believe that you are worth every penny of the money you make. Shooting for $100,000 is undoubtedly a significant mental leap if you consider yourself to be a $30, 000 per year employee. Be prepared to make the essential professional and life decisions to improve your ability to generate more money personally. If you are certain that you are worth more than what you are now earning, you should take the required actions to change your situation and get more control over your money rather than "settling" for a job that merely provides for your family's needs.

86. Make the decision to develop your career based on earning possibilities.
We all work for money, that much is a universal truth. Additionally, as you are already aware, there

are some jobs that pay more without requiring you to put in additional, physically taxing work hours. Generate sure to pick a career where you can earn more if your main driving force is to make more money. Establish your objectives and take the appropriate actions to advance in your profession.
87. Spend some time examining your credit report. Many individuals are unaware that one of the quickest methods to save a few thousand dollars is to check your credit score and correct errors on your report. You may possibly save thousands of dollars annually on interest rates by taking the time to raise your credit score.

88. By blogging, you can earn money.
Blogging is an excellent way to get extra money if you have free time. Despite the fact that you won't receive any money right now, you can potentially earn a respectable salary after a few months of diligent work. Securing a good domain name and obtaining hosting services are the first steps to taking before setting up your blog.

89. Review products in writing.
There are numerous websites online that will pay you a little sum of money for writing product reviews. This might be a fantastic side gig for you if you have a quick and informed writing style.

90. Stage residences.

You can assist folks in selling their homes by staging it for a rapid sale in light of the rising number of people selling homes and coping with the all too real danger of foreclosure. Offer your services if you have a talent for design.

91. At least a week's worth of meals should be planned out, and the menu plan should serve as the basis for your grocery list.
This will not only help you save time, energy, and money, but it will also make it much simpler for you to stick to a better eating plan rather than giving in to the temptation of fast food and processed goods.

92. Remove yourself from your computer.
The online world has created a virtual environment that is alive with diversions. Make an effort to do the vast majority of your work offline to improve productivity.

93. Consider purchasing a Tivo if you enjoy watching TV.
If you want to effectively reduce a one-hour television program to 40 minutes, think about using DVR or Tivo.

94. Choose to set up automatic bill payment.
You'll save time processing payments and visiting payment centers by using an automated method.

You also get rid of the interest rate increases for late payments as well as the late fees.

95. Recognize useful keyboard shortcuts.
Having a good understanding of keyboard shortcuts will help you save a lot of time. Try learning shorter keyboard instructions like Ctrl + S to save, etc. This is especially helpful if your line of work necessitates frequent computer use.

96. Make the decision to rise earlier.
You can complete your duties in a quarter of the time by doing them when everyone else is asleep and the house is still silent. If you have young children running about, which makes it nearly hard to carry out a thorough cleansing, this is a highly practical answer.

97. Every time it's feasible, decide to shop online.
You can reduce the amount of time you spend shopping, the amount of money you spend on petrol, and the amount of impulsive buying you do by choosing to shop online rather than rummaging through racks upon racks of apparel, shoes, or any other consumer goods. This is a sensible choice that is especially beneficial over the holidays. Do your shopping online if you don't particularly enjoy the idea of joining the other few hundred shoppers.

98. By purchasing a broadband connection, you can invest in speeding up your Internet. It only makes sense to make sure you have a strong, dependable connection if your ability to access the internet is essential to your ability to do your job and be productive.

99. Make an effort to increase your typing speed. By speeding up your typing, you can significantly reduce the amount of time it takes to do any work that involves encoding, including producing emails, articles, and just about any other type of document.

100. Install Caller ID so you can save time by not making pointless phone calls.
Avoid making unnecessary calls so that they don't keep you from working.

Conclusion

It's not necessary to be extremely clever to earn more money and be successful, as you may have learned from the advice given. You do not need to be the creator of the next breakthrough technology poised to unseat Facebook. Additionally, it is not necessary to be a celebrity or a rocket scientist to make your own riches. Instead of concentrating on lofty objectives, examine your regular daily operations and look for creative ways to save time and money. Success, once more, is the culmination of all these little things.

Make an effort to adopt sensible routines and a simple way of living. You don't require all those accoutrements to boast about your accomplishments or boost your self-esteem. Make the decision to streamline, alter, and erase your life. Avoid activities that just squander your time and money and instead look for worthwhile pursuits.
You'll discover that by making minor adjustments to your routine, viewpoint, and approach to life and possessions, you may actually reduce wasteful spending and free up more of your time. In reality, learning to spend less and

concentrating on your abilities are the keys to increasing your income. Consciously decide not to complicate things and stay away from pointless distractions that divert your attention from your objectives.

Once you've accomplished all of this, you'll discover that the rewards are quite encouraging.

www.ingramcontent.com/pod-product-compliance
Lightning Source LLC
LaVergne TN
LVHW052108160826
845678LV00015B/3425